Old Bo'ness
Alex F. Young

Designed by Ebenezer Simpson of Stirling (1854-1934) and sculpted by J & G Mossman of Glasgow, the Jubilee Fountain in Market Square, replacing the 1818 St. John's Well, was gifted to the town by James Allan of the grain merchants J & J Allan to celebrate Queen Victoria's Golden Jubilee in 1887, and Allan's third year as the town's Chief Commissioner. Standing 11 feet 6 inches high, including the Wenham gas lamp, the latest in lighting technology and gifted by the Bo'ness Gas-light Company, it was fashioned from grey Argyllshire granite with red Peterhead granite basins. The men are John Paul (1825-1903), clerk to the parish council, John Mackay, James Dymock (1826-1910), ship's chandler of Ainslie's Land at East Quay, William Donaldson (1842-1925), ship broker and timber merchant, John S Jeffrey, watchmaker, and Neil Livingston.

First Published in the United Kingdom, 2009
Stenlake Publishing Limited
54-58 Mill Square, Catrine, KA5 6RD
www.stenlake.co.uk

ISBN 9781840334821

INTRODUCTION

Writing of his visit to Bo'ness in the summer of 1787, the poet Robert Burns described it as that *dirty, ugly place*, but as his century passed into the 19th, the dirt would generate the prosperity to sweep away the ugliness.

The opening of the new dock in 1881 brought such an increase in trade, through the export of coal and the import of Scandinavian wood for pit pops, that by 1901 the town was on the crest of an economic wave.

There were new public buildings, parks, modern housing, and new hope. The future, however, was to be industrial decline, and the difficult transformation to a post-industrial community. No better, no worse, just different.

ILLUSTRATION ACKNOWLEDGEMENTS

Bo'ness Town Trust Association; Front Cover, 1, 4 (lower), 5, 8 (both), 10 (inset), 22 (lower), 23, 26 (lower), 29 (lower), 30, 31 (both), 32, 33 (lower), 34, 35 (both), 38 (both), 39, 42, 43 (both), 47 (centre), 50 (lower), 51 (upper), 56 (lower), 59 (both), 60 (both), 62 (upper), 63 (upper), 76 (lower), 78 (both), 79 (upper), 82 (upper), 83 (upper), 84, 86 (upper), 87, 88 (lower), 89 (upper), 90, 91 (both), 91 (both), 92, 93 (lower), 94, 95 (both), 96 (both). **The Bo'ness Journal**; 7, 24 (lower), 29 (upper), 41, 47 (upper), 55 (lower), 75 (lower), 88 (upper both), 89 (lower both), 93 (upper). **Falkirk Council Archives**; 17 (both), 27 (lower), 31 (lower), 51 (upper), 58 (upper), 77, 87 (upper), 92 (lower). **Robert Grieves**; Inside back cover (lower). **Tom Heaviside**; 73 (upper). **Guthrie Hutton**; 63 (upper), 64/65, 66 (both), 67 (both). **Wolfgang Mohr**; 45 (headstones). **Robin Nelson**; 21/22 (upper), 69 (lower), 70/71 (lower), 71 (upper), 72 (upper). **Stuart Sellar**; 19 (lower), 20 (lower), 21 (lower), 68 (both), 69 (upper both), 73 (lower). **Robert Spowart**; 45 (upper left), 61, 86 (lower). **The George Waugh Collection**; 5 (upper), 55 (upper), 85 (both). **W Douglas Yuill**; 14 (lower), 15, 16 (both), 80 (upper).

BIBLIOGRAPHY

Francis H Groome, *Ordnance Gazetteer of Scotland: A Survey of Scottish Topography, Statistical, Biographical and Historical*, Thomas C Jack, Edinburgh, 1885.
Richard Jaques, *Falkirk and District (Architecture)*, The Rutland Press, 2001.
Don Martin, *The Monkland & Kirkintilloch and Associated Railways*, Strathkelvin District Libraries, 1995.
William Maxwell, *The History of Co-operation in Scotland*, Scottish Section of the Co-operative Union, 1910.
Thomas J Salmon, *Borrowstouness and District*, William Hodge & Co., 1913.
Rev Kenneth McKenzie, *The New Statistical Account of Scotland, vol. 2, County of Linlithgow, Parish of Borrowstouness*, 1843.
Colin McWilliam, *The Buildings of Scotland; Lothian and Edinburgh*, Penguin, 1978.
Rev Robert Rennie, *The Statistical Account of Scotland, vol. 18, Parish of Borrowstouness*, 1791-1799.
The Royal Commission on Ancient Monuments and Historical Monuments and Constructions of Scotland. 10th Report – Counties of Midlothian and West Lothian, Edinburgh, 1929.
The Railway Magazine, February, 1910.
Miles K Oglethorpe, *Scottish Collieries – An Inventory of the Scottish Coal Industry in the Nationalised Era*, Royal Commission on the Ancient and Historical Monuments of Scotland, 2006.
W. A.C. Smith, *The Lothians' Last Days of Steam*, Stenlake Publishing Ltd, 2005.

ACKNOWLEDGEMENTS

Dido Bohlen, Hans Bohlen, Miss Elizabeth Bryce of Bo'ness Amateur Operatic Society, Rev David R Bunyan of St Catharine's Church, Sybil Cavanagh of West Lothian Local History Library at Blackburn, Falkirk Council Archives, Callendar House, Falkirk, Robert Grieves, Klaus Grupe, George and Douglas Haston, Guthrie Hutton, Thomas Johnston, Rick Jones at *www.oldclassiccar.co.uk*, Capt Alex McNee and the Salvation Army at Bo'ness, Margaret Meldrum, Wolfgang Mohr, Robin Nelson, Ian Osborough of West Lothian Golf Club, Angus Smith and Bo'ness Town Trust Association, Douglas 'Douggie' Sneddon, Robert Spowart, Jeff Stewart of Bo'ness Fair Festival, W Douglas Yuill, The Scottish Fisheries Museum, St Ayles, Anstruther and The Scottish Mining Museum, Lady Victoria Colliery, Newtongrange.

The westward view along Corbiehall with the Old Kirk on Panbrae Road above, photographed between the construction of the Thomson Place building, with Baxter the hairdresser's premises (in 2009 the Ashbank Veterinary Centre), in 1905, and the building of Catherine Place, beyond, in 1908. Robert Baxter, a native of Dalkeith, had started his hairdressing business at 43 North Street before moving here, but by 1908 it was Janet Baxter's confectionery shop. The crow-step gabled, pantile-roofed, building on the left, and those beyond, were demolished in 1932 for the council houses of 'Coffin Square' (43-51 Corbiehall) designed by local architect Matthew Steele.

Corbiehall from the west, around 1951. On the right is Dorothy Marshall's sweetie shop, which had been Baxter's, taking a delivery. Beyond is 'Coffin Square', a cul-de-sac of two 'L' shaped blocks flanking a central, rectangular block. The line of sight then passes the Star Cinema, the Church Wynd junction and into Seaview Place. Parked at its terminus on the left is an Alexander's 'Bluebird' bus.

The north side of Corbiehall around 1905, with the Masonic Hall and the Drill Hall – built in 1877 for the local volunteers, 'B' Company of the Linlithgowshire 2nd Rifle Volunteers, founded in 1857. By the time of this photograph, it was home to the 8th Volunteer Battalion, The Royal Scots (Lothian Regiment) (B Company) under the command of Captain Alexander Scott. Between the buildings, but hidden in this view, was the police station. The foundation stone of the Masonic Hall was laid by the Earl of Mar on 9th August 1884 and the hall opened the following January. In 1909 the Masonic order moved to new premises in Stewart Avenue and this building was purchased by the brewer Sir James Calder for the British Legion. By the 1920s there were financial difficulties and in July 1927 it was sold to the Salvation Army for £800.

George Ainslie & Son's Drill Hall Garage on the north side of Corbiehall in the 1970s, when a vintage car club rally had brought some welcome trade. The business was started by George Ainslie (1851-1928) and his son Thomas Waddell Ainslie (born 1887) in Grangepans, working on bicycles, then motorcycles, in a number of garage premises before taking the one adjoining the Clydesdale Hotel on Seaview Place. In March 1920 the premises was offered at public roup but failed to reach its upset price of £1,000. On the morning of Wednesday 1st November 1922 fire broke out at the rear of the hotel, consuming the kitchen and their garage, with the loss of one car. They bought the Old Drill Hall (built 1877 as the Volunteer Hall), here on Corbiehall, and converted it to a modern garage, with space for 20 cars, an inspection pit, electric plant for re-charging accumulators (batteries) and five cars for hire. After service in the Great War, as a sergeant in the army's heavy tractor section, Thomas returned to take over the running of the business from his father. He died at his home, 18a Braehead, in August 1948 and his nephew, George Dundas, ran the business until 1980 when it was bought by Douglas and Robert Haston.

Opposite: Bo'ness Salvation Army Corps' 'Home League', photographed outside their citadel (the old Masonic building) in Corbiehall for an illustrated feature article in the 'War Cry' edition of 6th March 1937. The League was inaugurated in January 1907, when the first branch opened at Cambridge Heath in London.

In the years since, memories may have faded a little, but the following faces and names are recalled:
Front row: unknown, Mrs McCluskey, Mrs Queenan and Mrs Morrison (secretary).
Second row: Mrs Mary Scotland (nee Ballantyne), Mrs Morrison, Mrs Bell, unknown, Mrs Paton, Angie Buchanan, unknown, Mrs Scotland, Jess Simpson and Mrs Scotland.
Third row: Mrs Bell, unknown, unknown, Mrs Laken, Mrs Sanderson, unknown, unknown, Mrs Ash, Mrs Ash and unknown.
Back row: Mrs Chalker, Bab Kidd (nee Simpson), Mrs Carr, unknown, Mrs Smith, unknown, unknown, May Spowart, Mrs Murphy, Bethia Brown, unknown, Mrs Bow and Mrs Logan.
On the right is the Corps Officer, Captain Ronald Rowntree Chalker, who resigned from the 'Army' in the early 1950s and settled in Rochdale, Lancashire where he started a fruit and vegetable business, which still trades as Ron Chalker (The Potato Man) Ltd.

Left: Seaview Place, with the Clydesdale Hotel on the left, running to Church Wynd before opening onto Corbiehall which sweeps round to terminate with the parish church on Panbrae above. The woman with the babe in arms is passing the petrol pump outside Ainslie's garage.

Below: The 720 seat Star Cinema, built on the site of the Episcopal church building, which had been the parish church until 1888, on Corbiehall. Operated by Lothians Star Theatres Ltd, it opened on Christmas Night 1919 when, under the management of Mr S C Thurston, a distinguished audience were kept on the edges of their seats with a showing of *Sporting Life* – a love drama, woven around the Epsom Derby, with an exciting replica race and a glove fight until, as hoped, wedding bells rang out and virtue triumphed. On Mondays and Saturdays the programme ran from 1.30 pm and from Tuesday to Friday from 5.00 pm. Prices at this time were 5d. and 1/9d, with the films, distributed by FTS (Great Britain) Ltd, changing twice weekly. The cinema closed, following a three day showing of *The Night of the Generals*, on Saturday 27th May 1967. It is now (2009) used by the removals and storage company, *Re-Moov-It*.

Left: In this 1891 photograph of the town from Panbrae, Corbiehall is in the centre foreground taking the eye to the Clock Tower on North Street, from the footbridge over the railway line on the left. The building of this line in 1851 denied townspeople access to the foreshore and, under Admiralty rules, the Slamannan & Borrowstouness Railway were forced to build three of these bridges giving access to the 300 yard, twelve feet wide causeway they also built.

The dock gates, photographed from the harbour, at low tide.

Left: Work on the gateway of the new dock nearing completion in September 1881, photographed from the south quay, looking to the harbour. Trade through the port had been in decline since the 1860s, but this new dock, started in 1878 by the contractor Thomas Meik & Son of Edinburgh, would restore it. Covering seven and a quarter acres, and costing in the region of £200,000, (in 2007 equivalent to about £104m) the dock had a water depth of 22 feet, wharfage of 1200 feet and three hydraulic hoists each capable of loading 200 tons of coal per hour. The walls, 19 feet thick at the base and 38 feet high, were concrete – some 40,000 cubic yards of it – with a granite coping, standing on a base of 140,000 cubic feet of pitch pine. The 50 feet wide entrance was 120 feet long, and fitted with hydraulically operated gates of greenheart wood. It opened on Saturday 3rd December 1881, when the paddle steamer *William Muir*, carrying a party of dignitaries, broke the blue ribbon, to the strains of *Rule Britannia*. Close on the heels of the opening party came the 200 ton Norwegian brig *Eos*, to take on coal. The engineer Thomas Meik (1812-1896) had had the experience of similar work at Blyth, Burntisland and Ayr. In the spring of 1930 the gates' deteriorating wood was replaced.

The docks, photographed from the west side, looking towards Kinneil Street and the terraced housing on Union Street. The size of the boats berthed around the quay wall, a mix of working vessels and pleasure boats, reflects the tidal nature of the harbour and the necessity of building the new dock with its coal hoists, which can be seen above the buildings. Centre, is a Kinneil Collieries coal wagon.

The basic from the south side of the dock
gates showing the walkway across.

THE DOCKS.
BO'NESS.

One of the two large capacity, hydraulic, coal hoists at the east end of the docks loading the SS *Kenilworth*. These newer hoists could handle coal wagons of 30 tons gross and load 2,000 tons of coal per day. In 1909 a new, larger, hoist was installed, capable of loading 7,000 tons of coal per day. This photograph is undated but, on the night of Tuesday 30th January 1906, the *Kenilworth*, under Captain Scorgie and a crew of nine, was sailing, loaded with coal, from Bo'ness to Aberdeen when she struck rocks off Cove, south of Aberdeen, in a storm of sleet. With the steamer taking in water, they launched a dingy and landed at Nigg Bay, from where they walked back to Aberdeen. Within a few days the *Kenilworth* had broken up.

Right: The SS Glencairn in the dock around 1910. Built at Sunderland in 1889 by J Priestman & Co., for Livingston Connor & Co. of West Hartlepool, the 1174 ton Glencairn was bought by J Denholm & Co. of Bo'ness in October 1898; her first voyage for them being to Cronstadt in Russia, for wood. In 1912 she was sold, for £9,000, to Portugal and became the Victoria 2, and then in 1917 to Belgium where she was the Marcel. In November 1933, sailing out of Llanelly for Rouen, she ran aground close to the lighthouse. She was re-floated, but such was the damage that she was taken to the E G Rees shipyard at Llanelly and broken up.

Left: The docks, from the south quay, around 1923. In the foreground, under the bow of the *Oaklands*, is the 98 gross ton, 81 feet long, *Gluckauf* of Lubeck, a 'tjalk' or sailing coaster, which probably had come from Uleaborg in Finland, with pit props. Built in 1911 by L Mulder of Stadskanal in Friesland, Holland, she was registered at Lubeck from 1919 until April 1925 when she was sold to a company in Bremen. Her 60 horsepower engine was later increased to 90 horsepower, and in 1957 she underwent a reconstruction, lengthening her and adding to her height. She was laid up in 1967 and later scrapped. On the opposite quay is another German registered vessel, the 383 ton, three masted schooner, *Raymonde Naval* of Hamburg. Built in 1919 by J Smid & Son at Foxhol, Holland, she was bought in 1923 by Naval Reederei of Hamburg. A coastal trader with a crew of ten, she voyaged as far as North Africa. In 1927 she was renamed *Sissie* and in 1928 sold to the Atwater Shipping Company of Hamburg, before passing to Italian owners in 1931 and based at Rijeka in Croatia. She was bombed and sank in the Adriatic in 1944.

Left: Serving the Carron Co's cargo ship *SS Forth*, on the immediate left, are three of the company's lighters or barges of which, Nos. 10, 9 and 7 can be identified. Built by John Cran & Co at Leith in 1905, No. 10 was at Bo'ness until 1920 when she was sold to the Consett Iron Co at Durham. No. 9 was built at Glasgow by Barclay, Curle, and No. 7 was built at Grangemouth in 1866 for the Carron Co by Thomas Adams & Co. In 1923 she was sold to the Royal Gourock Yacht Club before being broken up in 1931. The *SS Forth*, built by A & J Inglis of Glasgow, and her sister ship the *SS Thames*, plied between the Firth of Forth and London carrying the Carron Co's products and general cargo.

The *SS Hunterfield* unloading Baltic timber at Bo'ness around 1909. She was built in 1903 by the Ailsa Shipbuilding Co. at Ayr for Love, Stewart & Co., the shipbrokers and commission agents of Kinneil Street, Bo'ness and served them until 1932, when she was sold to Marseille and re-named *Mairi Deftereou*. She had a difficult war. In June 1940 she grounded in the Rhone Estuary, damaging her rudder and propeller and was towed to Marseille, where she was seized and detained until going into Italian hands, and re-named *Genova*. In September 1943, back in Marseille, she was seized by the Germans and named *Diana* and was sunk by the Royal Navy submarine *HMS Untiring*, off the Italian port of Oneglia, on 12th April 1944.

Left: The Carron Co's ship *SS Thames* steaming out of Bo'ness on its weekly cargo trip to London which from June 1897 also carried passengers. She was built by A & J Inglis of Pointhouse Yard on the Clyde at Glasgow in 1887 (her sister ship, the *SS Forth* had been completed at the same yard the previous year). Both ships were lengthened by adding midship sections in 1906-07. Returning from London on 26th May 1918, she was torpedoed six miles off Seaham Harbour on the Durham coast by the *Unterseeboot* UC 17, under the command of Oberleutnant Nikolaus Freiherr von Lyncker, sinking with the loss of her master, W A McPhail, and three crewmen: Chief Officer John McKinnon (41), Able Seaman Richard Lane Winser (30) of the Royal Naval Volunteer Reserve, Plymouth, and Fireman Hamilton Ogg (36) of Leith. The company lost two other ships to submarine action during the war – the *Avon*, mined and sunk in the Thames Estuary on 9 April 1916, and the *Forth*, sunk four miles south west of the Shipwash Lightship, off the Suffolk coast.

A view of the dock, looking east, in 1925 showing three of the hydraulic coal hoists. The ship on the right appears to be moored to the centre buoys, whilst, judging by the height of her Plimsol Line above the water, the one by the east quay is waiting to be loaded.

The single screw bucket dredger *SS Almond* with one of the barges used to carry the dredgings out to the Forth for dumping. 136 feet long, 30 feet wide and with a gross tonnage of 309 she was built by Fleming and Ferguson at Paisley for the North British Railway Company's use at Bo'ness and launched in December 1914. She spent her working life in the Forth and was broken up in the 1960s.

Three fishermen working on a drift net at the dockside sometime early in the last century were the last of the few at Bo'ness. Migratory herring shoals were found in the Forth in 1794-95 but did not return, and although there were haddock, cod and skate, the *New Statistical Account* (1840) reported that there was a problem finding suitable bait (before the use of nets, fish were caught on long lines of baited hooks). In the 1880s, there were 26 registered fishing boats, employing 103 men, but by 1910 the *Fisherman's Almanac* records that this number had fallen to ten, and by 1920 to five – *Memento, Agnes, Peggy, Heather Bell* and the *President Garfield*. The last registered boat to bear the port's letters, 'BO', was BO15, the *Heather Bell*.

The 48 feet fishing boat LH437, the *Ros Corr*, left in the harbour by a receding tide in the late 1960s. She was built at John Tyrell's boatyard at Arklow in County Wicklow in 1952 (Irish registration no. D331), where Sir Francis Chichester's *Gipsy Moth III* was also built. From November 1965 she was a prawn trawler with Arthur K B Clarkson of Leith until sold in 1975 to become a houseboat at Blyth in Northumberland.

The Clydesdale Hotel, seen here in Seaview Place in 1898 with its public bar on the corner of Church Wynd, took its name from the Clydesdale Bank which had previously occupied the site. Today's roundabout, with its capstan, is many years off. The hotel was owned by Hugh Clark (born in Roslin 1843), but following his death in 1899 it was auctioned in Edinburgh in March 1900 at the upset price of £3,500. The annual turnover was given as 820 gallons of spirits and 132 hogsheads (7,128 gallons or 57,024 pints)) of beer. Following good competition it was knocked down to Clark's son, James, for £5,400. With the new owner came change and an almost complete rebuild. During the Second World War, when it was the town council offices, the basement was reinforced for use as an ARP (Air Raid Precautions) shelter.

This view of Seaview Place, looking to North Street, was taken in the 1920s after completion of the alterations to the Clydesdale Hotel, by this time Jeffrey's Hotel. In April 1924 the town council bought the building from Mrs Jeffrey for the bargain price of £3,000 and converted it to their municipal chambers. The advertising board on the gable wall to the left is for Elizabeth Norval's Restaurant and Coffee Rooms, which were owned by the town council, at 47 North Street and was intended to catch the eye of passengers disembarking at the railway station. Elizabeth was a daughter of Alex Norval, the grocer in North Street; she ran the restaurant with her sisters Jane and Ann, and ended her days at Kelso in 1939, aged 71 years.

This view of the railway station in September 1955 with the 5.20pm train to Polmont at the platform, as a locomotive with coal wagons passes through, from the harbour side, shows the clock tower and the buildings in North Street to the left and the burgh chambers (previously Jeffrey's Hotel) to the right. The passenger train locomotive, No. 67494, was a C16 class, based at St. Margaret's Sheds in Edinburgh and one of a series of 21 built for the North British Railway Company as their class 'L' model, between 1916 and 1921. They would all be out of service by 1961, this one being the last to survive.

The railway station from west of the signal box behind Corbiehall in May 1960. The locomotive is a Class 3P-G 4-4-0, built in 1916 at the Caledonian Railway Works at St Rollox in Glasgow for the Caledonian Railway. She was withdrawn from service in October 1961, having latterly been based at Motherwell, and scrapped in August 1963. The people on the track are not anxious travellers looking for the platform, but members of the Stephenson Locomotive Society on a visit during an enthusiasts' railtour.

This locomotive, a 4F-A type No. 43141, built at British Railways' Doncaster Works in 1951 and based at Polmont, was the last passenger train, the 6.50pm for Polmont, waiting to leave Bo'ness Station on 5th May 1956. Shortly after the closure of Bo'ness, it was transferred to Normanton, south east of Leeds, and when withdrawn from service in November 1966 was broken up at Hull. Beyond the station fence is Seaview Place and Providence Brae.

Locomotive 67472, a 4-4-2T class C15, in British Railways livery, at Bo'ness on 3 December 1955, then based at Hawick, was one of 30 of the model built by the Yorkshire Engineering Company of Sheffield for the North British Railway between 1911 and 1913. Weighing 69 tons and 15 cwt, her four drive wheels had a diameter of 5 feet 9 inches.

These locomotives at Bo'ness in November 1962 were waiting to be scrapped. With the introduction of diesel locomotives under the British Railways Modernisation Plan, steam locomotives were taken out of service faster than contractors could break them up, and Bo'ness was used to hold those awaiting their fate. The last steam locomotive in the Scottish Region was withdrawn on 1st May 1967. At the front of the line is No. 40158 (formerly LMS No. 158), a 2-6-2T, from Dawsholm Shed, Glasgow, built at the London, Midland & Scottish Railway works at Derby in October 1937 (with 138 others of the same type). In 1948 she was based at Southport in Lancashire before going to Dawsholm, Glasgow, working the Glasgow Central Low Level service connecting Balloch and Maryhill with Rutherglen and Coatbridge. Withdrawn from service in January 1962, she was scrapped at Connel's yard at Calder, Lanarkshire in April 1963. They scrapped 47 other locomotives at this time. Second in line is No. 67619, a 2-6-2T LNER Class IV from Helensburgh Shed from where she ran to Airdrie on the Glasgow Queen Street Low Level Line.

North Street, where Scotland Street branches left at the Journal and Gazette building, around 1904. On the left are the premises of the Glasgow born grocer and spirit dealer, Alexander Norval (1832-1915).

The view down Providence Brae or Providence Lane as it was once known. According to Thomas J Salmon's book, *Borrowstouness and District*, the name derives from its many hiding places from the press gangs that visited the town in early times.

This view of North Street, looking north west from Market Square, shows the Jubilee Fountain, the clock tower, the Douglas Hotel and East Pier Street. On the right corner is James Dymock the grocer (and ship's chandler) and part of Walker & Johnstone, the draper's 'Market House' shop. This corner building was destroyed by fire on Wednesday, 11th October, 1911. The clock tower's chequered history was the result of the town's early mining wealth. In 1778 Douglas, the 8th Duke of Hamilton, gifted a replica of Inveraray Castle as a prison and courthouse with a school in the attic, but due to subsidence it was a ruin before it opened and was only ever used as a grain store. It was demolished in the 1870s but the clock tower was preserved and re-erected as seen here. The current town clock was erected in 1984.

Market Square, around 1903. looking east along North Street with Walker & Johnstone, the drapers and clothiers, Market House premises on the right. The Jubilee Fountain in Market Square, replaced the 1818 St. John's Well, was gifted to the town by James Allan of the grain merchants J & J Allan to celebrate Queen Victoria's Golden Jubilee in 1887, and Allan's third year as the town's Chief Commissioner.

The grain merchant and benefactor to the town, James Allan of Messrs J & J Allan was born at Coatdyke, Old Monkland, Lanarkshire in 1833, where his father was an iron contractor and came to Bo'ness, with his older brother John, in the 1850s. They were enterprising and became mining contractors to the Kinneil Iron Works, before branching into potatoes and grain when they became classed as merchants. They also bought properties and prospered. In August 1858, aged 24 years, he married nineteen year old Helen Kinloch (died 1910). He became involved in public affairs, joining the town trust and becoming a commissioner (town councillor) and finally commissioner (provost). In his latter years he suffered from 'weakness of the heart', blamed on a fall from a horse, and his death, at Viewforth House on 10th September 1904, aged 71 years, was not unexpected.

North Street, looking east, around 1904, with the clock tower and the Douglas Hotel on the left and 'Ye Old Anchor Tavern' to the right. As part of the renewal and redevelopment of this corner, the Anchor Tavern was built in 1891 by the Edinburgh builder, Arthur Colville, for the brewer Thomas Usher & Sons of Edinburgh, and was tenanted, initially, by the 55 year old retail spirit merchant, Charles Galbraith, also of Edinburgh. By 1901 he, with his Leith born wife Alice (nee Newcater) and their three children (James, Alice and Charles), had returned to the city.

Market Square from the East Pier Street junction with North Street, looking along Market Street (once Beaton's Close), past the Jubilee Fountain, towards South Street with the Clydesdale Bank, opened in March 1905, on the right. Built of red sandstone from Locharbriggs Quarry in Dumfriesshire, the three storey building was designed by the Glasgow architects J W Thomson (who died weeks before the opening) and John Baird, and built by local builder Messrs Jipps & Sneddon. William Swan, its first agent, died in November 1908. The bank closed in February 2005. Looking to South Street, the large building was mainly occupied by the Union Bank of Scotland Ltd, with William Elliot the grocer, at street level, to the right.

This view of North Street, looking east from Market Square, dates from around 1905. Walker & Johnstone had moved their Market House shop across the street in May 1901. Under the shadow of the Cross Keys building is the apparently tiny premises of W W Broome (William Wedgwood Broome) the stationer, printer and publisher of the *Bo'ness Journal*, founded by his father Francis W Broome in 1878. William was a compositor with the paper, before working with Fife newspapers and returning to Bo'ness as editor. He died in May 1925 aged 69 years.

A draper's shop with its proprietor, possibly Alex Wallace, outside his premises at No. 25. North Street – the shadows suggest that it was on the north side - in the 1890s. The crowd is more likely to have been drawn by the photographer than the bargains displayed in the window, which include a man's suit for 15/6*d*.

John Johnston the baker and confectioner was born in Bo'ness in 1848, the son of the haulage contractor Peter Johnston. He married Catherine Stevens at Polmont, in July 1872, and their first child, Peter, was born at Cardross, Dunbartonshire the following year. Returning to Bo'ness in 1879 he started his bakery business in premises where the Hippodrome Cinema would later stand, moving to larger premises in North Street around 1884. He retired in 1920, leaving his son James, and son in law Peter MacPherson, to carry on, and died at his home, Dalhousie, on Panbrae Road on 17 July 1934, aged 85 years. The advert dates from around 1925.

Johnston's Fiat van with (probably) his son-in-law Peter M MacPherson standing in front. His daughter, Catherine Hamilton Stevens Johnston, (born 1885), had married 34 year old MacPherson, an Edinburgh based commercial traveller, at Edinburgh in November 1914, bringing him into the business. They both died in Edinburgh in 1962.

Opposite upper: Standing out against the dark stonework of the Hamilton Arms in this view of North Street from the east around 1936 is a General Post Office telephone kiosk. If it followed the national pattern, the first in Bo'ness was probably outside the post office building. Of concrete construction and painted white, the 'K3' design kiosk was introduced in 1929, and intended for, 'sites of special architectural importance, scenic localities and for general outdoor use in rural and urban areas'.

Right: This Alexanders Stores advertisement from August 1910 tempts 'now that the nights are creeping in …' offering 'cheaper by the dozen' gas lighting accessories; upright burners, mantles and globes. This branch and those at Kirkintilloch, Kilsyth, Falkirk, Glasgow and Ayr were administered from a head office in Bath Street, Glasgow.

Opposite lower: In the spring of 1959 there was still some rivalry on North Street between F & W Woolworth on the left and Alexanders Stores opposite. Franklin Winfield Woolworth opened his first "pile it high and sell it cheap" store in Utica, New York State in 1879 and his first in Britain, at Liverpool, in November 1909. By 1939 he had 757 others across the country. This branch closed on Saturday, 27 December 2008 as the chain, nationwide, went into administration. Adjacent to Alexanders is the Cross Keys public house, still with its 1909 frontage, designed by Matthew Steele.

Below: Dymock's Building on North Street was opened by Prince Charles on 2nd June 2004, following its restoration by the Pollock Hammond Partnership for the National Trust for Scotland and conversion to eight small flats for the Trust's Little Houses Improvement Scheme. In 1650 the Duke of Hamilton feued it to William Thomsoun and in 1720 it formed part of the dowry of Jean Gregorie when she married Thomas Dundas. In the early nineteenth century it came into the hands of Mr Dymock before being acquired by John Anderson, the philanthropist, in 1852 when it was used to process whale-oil. Now a commercial property, it was used, in succession, by the plumber, James Dymock & Sons, a motor cycle repair shop and a bakery.

Standing in the doorway of this confectioner's shop on the north side of South Street is thought to be its proprietrix Jessie Chalmers, a widow, (born in Glasgow around 1843), who lived in Hastie's Close on North Street with her daughters Margaret and Mary. The picture looks to the gable at the end of the Vennel (Market Street) in the 1890s. This was all swept away in August 1901.

Opposite: On Monday 12 August 1901, the contractor Jipps & Snedden started this demolition work in South Street as part of the renewal programme to clear away the old, the cramped and the decaying; the rubble in the foreground was once Henderson's building facing onto South Street. The building on the right, at ground level, stood on Beaton's Vennel and shows the line of the east side of today's Market Street – the four pot chimney stacked building survives on Market Place. The rubble was used to fill in an old pit shaft near the Green Tree Tavern on North Street.

A back court, thought to be somewhere in the old town in the 1890s, probably photographed by Alex Dufton of East Pier Street. Some have suggested that it is Black's dairy on School Brae, whilst others, using only part of the image, that it portrays Jessie Brown returning home with a bucket of water.

South Street looking east with the junction of Beaton's Vennel, or simply the Vennel, on the left.

Upper right: Beaton's Vennel (the future Market Street) going, on the right, to Market Square from South Street. The main building, with the clock tower above, sided onto a small unnamed square, and of the two shop premises one may have been Heggie the green grocer – it was demolished in the next phase of redevelopment. The area, extending to almost one acre, had held 87 houses with 356 occupants, fifteen shops, four stables and several bakehouses.

Lower right: Standing in an early 1900s building site, during the town's re-development are, from left to right: Robert Kilpatrick (1855-1915), slater and cement merchant of 101 North Street; Robert Simpson (1862-1936), joiner and builder, 64 South Street; T Yuill, of whom nothing is known, and Robert James Jamieson (1836-1910), solicitor, Town Clerk, Clerk to the Police Commissioners, Harbour Commissioners and the School Board.

South Street at the junction with Schoolyard Brae (later School Brae), is shown on the 1856 map as 'Site of Market Cross', and is seen here photographed in the 1890s. The premises of the wine and spirit dealer Thomas Findlay were subsequently demolished and rebuilt in 1900 as the Turf Tavern, and on the right, the shop of Alex. Steele, the grocer and spirit dealer, is today (2009) Morrisons, the bookmakers.

Upper right: This photo shows the Hope Tavern, W S Stratford, the wine and spirit merchant, at 27 South Street, photographed from School Brae, across the old Market Place, in the late 1890s, before the redevelopment created Hope Street (once Society Wynd and renamed in honour of Admiral Hope) and the present-day South Street. The man standing in the doorway may be Walter Stephen Stratford, born at Gravesend in Kent in 1871, who was orphaned and committed to the Merchant Seamen's Orphan Asylum in Hermon Hill, Wanstead, north east London, as an eight year old. Somehow he found his way to Bo'ness where, in July 1896, he married Agnes Robertson and died at Liberton Brae, Edinburgh in May 1922, aged 51 years. Immediately prior to its demolition the premises were occupied by Gideon Scott, also a wine and spirit dealer. The stairway on the left led to an enclosed courtyard within the buildings, flanked by Society Wynd and Gray's Lane.

Lower Right: Had Robert Renton the grocer and wine merchant, in the doorway of his shop on South Street in the 1890s, looked to his right he might have seen Walter Stratford as he was photographed in the doorway of the Hope Inn, next door. Born at 55 Engine Street, Bathgate in 1856, Robert's father William, a blacksmith, died in 1859. In 1882 he married Barbara Waddell and by the time of this photograph they were living at 4 Woodford Terrace, Bo'ness, with their three daughters; 16 year old Eliza, who assisted in the shop, Violet (14) and Barbara (11) who were at school. On special offer that week was 'Bottled Stout' at 2/- per dozen bottles, Bass Ale at 2/3 per dozen, finest Porter at 5*d* per quart and Mazawattee tea, then at the height of its popularity. He died at home, Effie Villa, Dundas Street in September 1925.

Left: South Street from the west, with the draper Nicol & Hill on the Hope Street corner on the left. The Turf Tavern at the School Brae opening on the right was built by Thomas Peattie of Knowe Park for James Aitken of Falkirk in 1900. This was part of the new building programme that swept away the Hope Tavern (replaced by the Market Tavern on the Market Street corner) and Renton the grocer and replaced it with the Anderson Building, on a site bought for £450, to drawings by architect James Thomson of East Pier Street. The 'Building' commemorated John Anderson (as did the Academy), and was financed by his bequest, administered by trustees. Anderson was born on 4 February 1795, the son of John Anderson, teacher, and his wife Jean Paterson, who had married in November 1793. The Census of 1841 shows him as a 45 year old grocer, living in South Street with his 70 year old mother and 40 year old sister, Margaret; both were cloth merchants. By 1861 their mother had died, but brother and sister were still together in the South Street house, looked after by a 16 year old servant, Catherine Dundas Cunningham from Carriden. He died, still unmarried, in the family home on 14th April 1870, when his occupation was given as banker.

Above: Bo'ness had been a post town since 1755, but in January 1911 the town council 'memorialised' the Post-Master General requesting that the town be raised to a head post office, quite separate from any other business. 63 year old David Taylor, the bookseller, stationer and newsagent at 59 South Street, was at that time a sub-post master to Linlithgow. The Post Office investigated and agreed but, to the surprise of the council members, who had wanted it sited on School Brae, chose the location seen in this 1913 photo on the corner of Union Street and East Pier Street. Building work began in May 1911. The architect was James Thomson of East Pier Street, the masonry work was undertaken by John Hardie & Son of Barn Yards, the joinery done by Robert Simpson of South Street, the slate and plasterwork by Robert Kilpatrick of North Street, and the plumbing by Charles Anderson of Kinneil Street. Without formal ceremony, it opened on Monday, 4 December 1911 staffed by the Postmaster, five sorting clerks and telegraphists, one telephonist, eight postmen, and three telegraph messengers. The new Postmaster, who would live on the top floor, two bedroom, house was George Macadie Weir. A native of Wick, where his father was a ropemaker, he had served in the telegraph office there, before moving to Aberdeen and then to Edinburgh for a 20 year spell in the telegraph office. He died at the age of 67 in the Royal Mental Hospital, Aberdeen, in January 1936. Here, he stands in front of the car.

Left: South Street, looking west, around 1912, with the Market Tavern on the Market Street corner.

Staff outside the Co-operative Society's shop in South Street in the early twentieth century. Founded in April 1861 by John Ramsay and a group of 20 men, it was funded by £1 shares – an initial payment of one shilling and thereafter 3d per week, with 5/- being the threshold for voting rights. Their first 'shop' opened on Saturday and Monday nights, with two of the committee acting as salesmen. The first night's takings amounted to £4.5s.4d, and their first trading year produced a turnover of £636, yielding a profit of £16 and earning the 55 members a dividend of 10d in the pound. Such was their growing success that a saleswoman was employed, working from 8.00am till 8.00pm Monday to Friday and 8.00am to 10.00pm on Saturdays – on a wage of 8/- per week. In 1908, sales of £76,847 earned the 1,752 members a dividend of 3/6 in the pound.

The Union Bank of Scotland's premises at 54 South Street in the late 1920s. An inscription on the photograph's mount, names the men as, from left to right, Marshall Upton, Provost Fred Livingston, H Johnson and Norrie Miller, but only Frederick J Livingstone (1883-1934), provost from 1931-1933, is known. Plans for the bank, by the architect James Thomson of East Pier Street, were submitted to the Dean of Guild Court in February 1900 by the solicitor and bank agent, John Marshall (1862-1921) – and passed. The three-storey building, looking down Market Street, consisted of the bank premises and a shop, Marshall's office on the first floor and two houses above. Today (2009) part of the building is occupied by P H Young & Co., solicitors, notaries and estate agents.

The Co-op's new Palladium lorry outside the coachbuilder James Porteous on Linlithgow's Bo'ness Road in 1922. Based in London's Putney, Palladium had started producing motor cars in 1912 and by 1914 had a range of commercial vehicles. By 1925 they were in financial difficulties and closed.

Town Hall, Bo'ness

The Town Hall and Library, with the bandstand in Glebe Park in 1905. When the town's commissioners bought the land for the town hall and the park in the 1890s the town's prosperity was on the rise, but by its completion, it was in decline. The plan submitted by the architects, Messrs Peddie and Washington Browne of Edinburgh - John More Dick Peddie (1853-1939) and George Washington Browne (1853-1921), was approved at the Dean of Guild Court on 14 October 1902, the town council having previously accepted the tender from Messrs Baikie and Peattie of Bo'ness for the building work. The total cost of £12,000, comprised of £5,000 from Andrew Carnegie for the library, £6,000 borrowed by the council and £1,000 from the Common Good Fund. The stone came from the town's Maidenpark Quarry and the cast iron would be of the very finest Yorkshire light grey pig iron of the second melting. Work would commence immediately and be completed by 31 March 1904 – with a penalty of £12 for each week of delay. The work was completed on time, and the opening was part of the Fair Day celebrations in the July. Part of the ceremony was the laying of the memorial stone by Mrs George C Stewart, beneath which was placed a glass jar containing copies of The Scotsman, Glasgow Herald, Bo'ness Journal and Linlithgow Gazette, a list of councillors and a copy of the council minutes bearing on the building, and one each of the coins of the realm. Also acknowledged was Mr George C Stewart (provost 1894-1903) for his gift of the north tower and its clock, and Mr James C Calder who had gifted the five chime bells. The clocks were supplied by Messrs H & R Millar, turret clock manufacturers of Castlebank Works, Edinburgh.

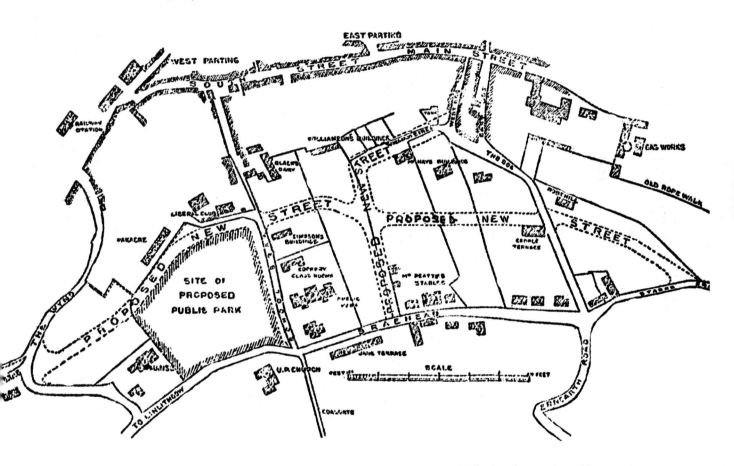

This early 1890s sketch shows the proposed new streets and public park, and was published at the opening of Stewart Avenue and the Glebe Park in 1900. The plan to build another road between Braehead and the West Bog was not followed through.

The bandstand in Glebe Park was supplied by Walter MacFarlane's Saracen Works in Glasgow, the commissioners having chosen the design from MacFarlane's extensive catalogue. From the terminal at the top, its slated roof, spandrels, columns and railings, the basic design could be adapted to form a bandstand, pavilion, summerhouse, arbour or kiosk. The burgh commissioners had acquired the ground in 1894 and in 1900 opened it as a public park. At this time the town hall was still on the drawing board. The bandstand's inaugural programme on Wednesday, 14 August 1901, was not without difficulty. The town had two bands, Bo'ness and Carriden Band, and Kinneil Band, and although they agreed to open the evening by playing the National Anthem together, neither wanted to play 'second fiddle' in the programme of music that followed. Who would be first? The town commissioners drew lots and Kinneil won – but they were not the "town's" band – and it was with reluctance that the Bo'ness and Carriden men joined them.

Right: The senior girls, and their teachers, at Bo'ness Academy in 1913 'captured' by the photographers D & W Prophet of Edinburgh and Dundee. The girls, so far, remain anonymous but the back of the photograph is inscribed, 'Mr Gladstone and Miss Ireland'. William Gladstone had been the school's headmaster since 1893 and retired in April 1917, only to die that September.

Stewart Avenue and its newly planted trees around 1906, with the Academy on the left and the Town Hall in the centre.

Right: Bo'ness Sea Scout Troop, founded at a meeting in the Burgh Court-House in November 1912, was one of many troops started around this time in coastal towns (and the first in Scotland), as an alternative to the Boy Scouts. Whilst Robert Baden-Powell was developing the Boy Scout movement, his older brother, Warington Baden-Powell, was promoting the Sea Scouts. John Jeffrey, who chaired the Bo'ness meeting, saw it as a training that would ...*turn the energies of youth into a channel, for lack of which they were now left to drift into all sorts of mischievous doings.* Thirty members were enrolled and Colonel Cadell of Grange promised to provide suitable premises. The following year, opening a sale of work (raising £25) in the Masonic Temple, the Rev T Ratcliffe Barnett, Scoutmaster of the St. Andrews (Church) Troop, suggested that excellent work for the boys would be the charting of the Firth of Forth, showing its mud banks. This photograph of 24 of the boys, with two rifles and a bugle, and their two leaders, would have been taken shortly after the troop's founding. Of the two officers in the centre, the one on the right is probably William McCurragh, the Scout Master. He was depute town clerk, and in 1915 commissioned into the Royal Naval Volunteer Reserve as a 2nd Lieutenant, serving in the Dardanelles from where he was invalided home. On returning to service, in spring 1917, he was attached to the 190th Machine Gun Company (R N V R) and killed at Arras on 27th May 1917. Aged 28 years, he left a widow, Annie Porteous.

The war memorial on Stewart Avenue, seen here in 1925, came about from an initial proposal, from a committee of town councillors and British Legion representatives, for a memorial in the form of a rugged cairn or cross at Bankhead, but was discarded for this site on Stewart Avenue, opened on Fair Day 1921. The architect George Simpson Barr (1891-1973) – of Galt & Barr, Glasgow – then of High Blantyre, who had designed the war memorial at Dunoon, was commissioned and produced this simple design of a 27 feet high pedestal of Portland stone – as are all war gravestones – with a bronze sword and a plaque listing the 398 townsmen who had been killed – *Salute the memory of these thy sons who fought & laid down their lives in the Great War.* It was unveiled by Lieut. Gen Sir Walter P Braithwaite, KCB (1865-1945), at a ceremony on Saturday 12th July 1924, when the guard of honour was formed of buglers and pipers of the 1st Battalion, the Kings Own Scottish Borders. Subscriptions, from employees of public works, residents and Bo'nessians from afar, amounted to £1347.16s.7d, and expenses to £1342.4/-, leaving a balance of £5.12s.7d, donated to the Bo'ness, Carriden and Kinneil Nursing Association. In September 1947 Provost David Lumsden unveiled the two plaques to those who were killed or died of their wounds in the Second World War – 95 servicemen and 22 merchant seamen.

In this 1934 view across the town from Douglas Park, the houses on the north side of Cadzow Crescent are in the foreground. One of them was home to local architect James Thomson. Standing above the tree-line can be seen the clock tower, the town hall and Craigmailen United Free Church. Houses were later built on the park side of the crescent.

Jim Henderson, son of John and Mary Henderson of Clydesdale Street, whilst a trombone player with Bo'ness Salvation Army Band. In 1942 he joined the Royal Scots but transferred to the 2nd Battalion of the Cameronians (Scottish Rifles) and saw action in Italy, Palestine and Belgium. On 21st April 1945, whilst advancing through Germany, he was killed by a shell-burst, near to Bleckede, south east of Hamburg – the same shell killing his pal, 33 year old Lance-Sergeant Andrew R Gray of the Unitas Buildings, Grangepans. They lie, within a few feet of each other, in Becklingen War Cemetery (section 18, C13 and D1), to the west of the road from Hamburg to Hanover, in north Germany, together with 2,372 other Commonwealth burials.

The headstone (left) to 20 year old Rifleman James Henderson in Becklingen War Cemetery (section 18, grave C13), Germany. Headstone (right) to Lance Serjeant Andrew Robertson Gray in Becklingen War Cemetery (section 18, grave D1), Germany.

St. Catharine's Episcopal Church and New Houses, Bo'ness

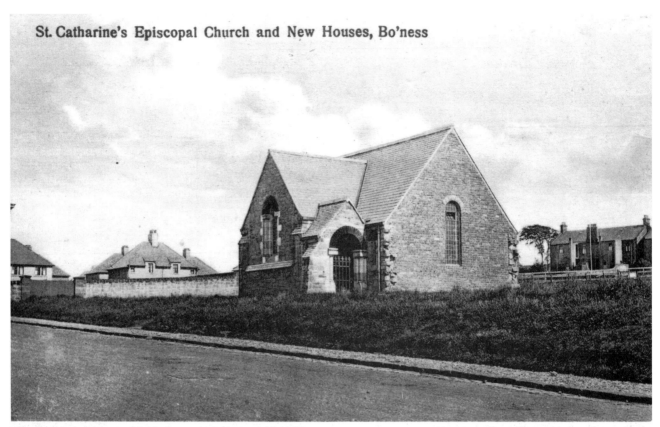

The foundation stone of St Catharine's Episcopal Church on Cadzow Crescent was laid on 8th January 1921 and the building dedicated in the December by the Rt Rev George Henry Somerset Walpole (1854-1929), the Episcopal Bishop of Edinburgh. The first congregation was formed in 1864 by the Rev R McLachlan of Armadale to serve the growing numbers of Episcopalians amongst workers from England and Ireland. In 1889 the congregation bought the old parish church on Corbiehall, vacated when the congregation moved to its new building on Panbrae Road. In 1919 it was sold to Lothians Star Theatres Ltd for their cinema and the Episcopalians used the town hall until the completion of this building. The hall to the rear was added in 1927. Today, the stark surroundings have been softened by an entrance gateway, steps, and mature trees.

Dean Road looking west from the Erngath Road junction, in or around 1932, and showing a mix of different house styles - from terraced cottages to 'four in a block' council houses. The rear gardens of the houses on the left backed onto the, then, burgh boundary.

Top: A sketch of the Infectious Diseases Hospital (or Fever Hospital) on Bo'ness Acres, off Dean Road, drawn at the time of its opening in July 1904. Built on two and a half acres of ground, granted by the Duke of Hamilton, it was designed by John Paxton Lawrie, the burgh engineer, and cost about £7,000. The double brick walls were harled on the outside and granite plastered on the inside, whilst the floor was of breeze concrete, supported on steel beams, with the floorboards laid on a spreading of asphalt. A cement skirting, with rounded corners, prevented the accumulation of dirt and microbes. The contractors were: brickwork, Messrs Jipps and Sneddon; joiner work, Mr Joseph Duguid; plaster and slater work, Mr William Templeton; painting and decorating, Mr David Grant; plumber work, Mr James Sinclair. It was demolished in 2000 to make way for the new hospital.

Centre: The main administration and living quarters at the hospital flanked by its pavilions around 1909. It consisted of four units: two pavilions – one for scarlet fever with sixteeen beds and one of eight beds for enteric fever and observation; a central building with bedrooms for five nurses, a matron, and two servants, a porter's room, matron's room, doctor's room, dispensary and general dining room. To the rear a laundry block also held discharge wards, an ambulance shed, mortuary, a disinfecting department (with a steam disinfector), wash-house and storerooms.

Bottom: Agnes Talman, Matron of the Fever Hospital, photographed in its grounds to mark her retiral in the spring of 1936. Born at Lethanhill, near Dalmellington, Ayrshire, on 9th December 1866, her father, John Talman, was manager of the Dalmellington Iron Mine Company Store. Trained at Glasgow's Royal Infirmary she came to Bo'ness in 1902, shortly before the opening of the new hospital. Despite looking a little stern, she was a competent nurse and administrator, and a well-known and liked figure in the community. She returned to Dalmellington and died there on 18th December 1960, aged 94 years. Her two eldest brothers, William and James McGill Talman died in the Great War.

Marchlands Avenue, looking to Marchlands Terrace, in the 1930s. With the old town centre becoming more and more decrepit this was one of a number of schemes built at the encouragement of the government to build *homes for heroes* in the years following the Great War. The new houses were of two, three, four and five bedroom design with electricity, running water, bathrooms, and front and rear gardens. By the spring of 1921 the first four houses were occupied by David Meldrum, clerk, John Arthur, music teacher, Agnes Binnie, married, and Jessie Mitchell, a widow. The next four would be tenanted by 31st August and the third batch by the following 15th May. The derivation of the name 'Marchlands' is uncertain. It may have come from its proximity to the old burgh boundary, or, from the house Marchlands on Grahamsdyke Road.

Chance Public Park (later renamed Kinglass Park), with its flagpole, looking to Grahamsdyke Road, was officially opened on Thursday, 18th August 1910 - its opening on Victoria Day (Tuesday, 24th May) having been cancelled due to the death of King Edward VII on 6th May. The honour of unfurling the inaugural flag was given to Annie Katherine Beatrix Thomson, the four year old daughter of Councillor William Gardner Thomson (of the timber merchants Thomson & Balfour Ltd). The site had been occupied by the bing of the coal and ironstone Chance Pit, which stood at the junction of Grahamsdyke Road and Gauze Road (named for Gaus House, which stood to the south). The town commissioners acquired the site from the trustees of the Duke of Hamilton, on a feu duty of £3 per annum in the 1890s, but not until 1909 was the work of clearing the bing undertaken by a staff of ten 'unemployed' workers. The outlay of £310.16s.2d, included fencing, shrubs and the forming of pathways, but was partly offset by a donation of £50 from Provost George C Stewart. The path on the right, with its mature trees, marks the old line of Gauze Road.

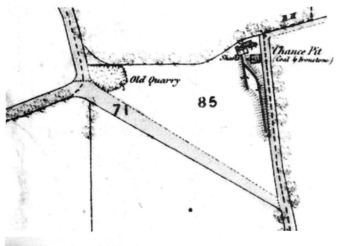

An 1850s plan of Chance Pit –showing the lines of the future Grahamsdyke Road, Kinglass Avenue and Gauze Road.

Grahamsdyke Road looking east, with children standing at the entrance to Chance Park on the right. The houses on the left were: *Thistlebank*, occupied by William Rankine, iron founder; *Benvue* (West and East), Thomas Wilks, customs officer and John C Liddle, solicitor; *Redlands*; William G Thomson, wood merchant; Mary Gordon, widow; Mary Ann S, Jessie C and Ida D Anderson, teachers; and James Anderson, Inland Revenue supervisor.

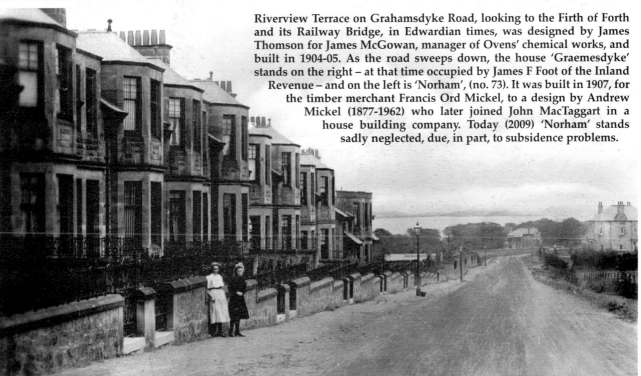

Riverview Terrace on Grahamsdyke Road, looking to the Firth of Forth and its Railway Bridge, in Edwardian times, was designed by James Thomson for James McGowan, manager of Ovens' chemical works, and built in 1904-05. As the road sweeps down, the house 'Graemesdyke' stands on the right – at that time occupied by James F Foot of the Inland Revenue – and on the left is 'Norham', (no. 73). It was built in 1907, for the timber merchant Francis Ord Mickel, to a design by Andrew Mickel (1877-1962) who later joined John MacTaggart in a house building company. Today (2009) 'Norham' stands sadly neglected, due, in part, to subsidence problems.

Grange Terrace with St Andrews United Free Church on the corner of Grahamsdyke Avenue, and Victoria Park on the right. Designed by J N Scott and A Lorne Campbell, it was styled on St Stephen's Church, Comely Bank, Edinburgh, and dedicated on 6th January 1906. It had cost £6,400.

Inset: Born at Kilbarchan , Renfrewshire in 1868, the Rev T Ratcliffe Barnett, Ph D (Edin), FSA (Scot) was educated at Glasgow University and Edinburgh Theological Hall and in 1900 married Maggie Muirhead of Glasgow. His first charge was at Fala, Blackshiels, Midlothian in 1899, before coming to Bo'ness in 1905 where he served until 1913 when he went to Greenbank Church in Edinburgh. He listed his recreations as walking, climbing and writing – his titles included; *The Dame of the Fine Green Kirtle* (1902), *The Road to Rannoch and the Summer Isles* (1924) and *The Cradle of Christianity* (1936). He died at Morningside, Edinburgh in 1946.

A nineteenth century watercolour of Grange House, flanked by cultivated ground and trees, and looking out to the hills of Fife. In his book *Borrowstounness and District*, Thomas J Salmon writes; The house, according to the date over the doorway, was built in 1564, and the initials on the pediments of the windows indicated Sir John Hamilton as its first proprietor. Grange Estate extended to about 350 acres and the name, it is said, derives from it having been the grange or farm to a settlement of monks attached to Culross. After the Reformation it fell to the Hamiltons and was called Grange-Hamilton, with its entrance driveway running from what is now Grange Loan. The vaulted basement contained the kitchen whilst the upper floors each had three rooms. In the early nineteenth century it was abandoned as a dwellinghouse and used as a dairy farm until around 1898 when it finally became too dangerous for habitation.

Four young children on Grange Loan, now Grange Terrace, during the demolition of Old Grange House in 1906. The house at No. 62 Grange Terrace, 'Bemersyde' was built on the site.

The east end of Grange Terrace, around 1909, with the house 'Bemersyde' (named perhaps after the 16th century house near Newton St Boswells) on the right, as it sweeps into Grange Loan. Bemersyde was occupied by plumber James H Sinclair who died in 1911 and his wife, Margaret Agnes Grant Sinclair. Grange School opened in August 1907.

Philpingstone Road around 1910, looking to the conspicuous Bridgeness Tower, which was built of Bo'ness brick around 1750 as a windmill to drive a Cadell pit pump and was later converted to a house.

Although this early 1890s photograph is captioned 'Grangepans from Victoria Park', it pre-dates the 'park' by a year or two. The paths are there, but in the bottom right corner we see the Barrel Well, later, perhaps, the source of supply for the Victoria Fountain and the adjacent drinking fountain.

The gas works with its square chimney and gasometer on Links Road, photographed from Grange Terrace across Stark's Brae. The manufacture of gas in the town dates from May 1844, and the name of the company, Bo'ness Coal Gas Light Company, tells us its use – no cooking or heating. In 1896 it became the Bo'ness Gas Light Company and in 1897, due to increasing demand, installed the new gas holder seen here, abandoning the one at Corbiehall. Erected by R & J Dempster of Manchester at a cost of £5,720, the new gasometer had a capacity of 100,000 cubic feet – the town then used 90,000 cubic feet per day – and scope for expansion through additions to the telescopic design. In 1949, through Nationalisation, the works became part of the Scottish Gas Board, and the gasometer remained in use until 1999.

Above: Grangepans from Victoria Park photographed, judging by the immaturity of the plants around the fountain, shortly after its opening in 1897. The line of buildings on the left formed the south side of Thirlstane Road as it ran east to Bridgeness, with the head gear of Pit No. 4 standing out above the smog.

Top left: The town, and its industries, from Victoria Park. In front of the woman and the little girl can just be seen the drinking fountain, also supplied from the spring of water, whilst directly behind them is New Grange Iron Foundry.

A contemporary drawing of Provost George C Stewart's Victoria Park ceramic fountain. It was not a popular choice, in either design or material, and in his speech presenting the fountain to the town said – *I have heard it said that the fountain is the only ugly thing in connection with this little nook, the basin and rockery being all right*. And in reference to the delicate nature of the ceramic – *My one fear is that, unless our boys give up the spirit of mischief, which so largely dominates them, damage may be done to this more brittle material by stone throwing*. How right he was.

Left: Toddlers at the Victoria Park fountain in the summer of 1913. As the town had celebrated Queen Victoria's Golden Jubilee in 1887 by accepting the drinking fountain in Market Square so, in 1897, they celebrated her Diamond Jubilee by naming this new nine acre park, Victoria Park and accepting from Provost George Cadell Stewart (1845-1913) the Doulton ceramic, 'Jubilee Fountain'. The railing was supplied by Alexander Callender of Bathgate, the lowest of six tenders, at 9*d*. per linear yard. There was, however, one small hitch on opening day, Tuesday, 22nd June – the Doulton factory at Lambeth in south London had dispatched the fountain by rail, instead of by steamer as requested, and it arrived too late for the ceremony, leaving the day to be celebrated with the planting of the 'Jubilee Clump' of trees. The fountain was inaugurated as part of the Fair celebrations in the July.

Left: A party of officials and employees photographed in the engine-room of the Electricity Works in Main Street at its opening in February 1905. Having obtained a provisional order from the Board of Trade in June 1903, the town council engaged the National Electric Construction Company to build the works, consisting of a boiler house, an engine room, a battery room and a test room, at a total cost of £25,000. There were two water-tube boilers by Messrs Heenan & Froude of Worcester, two high speed engines by Messrs Davey, Paxman & Co. of Colchester, and dynamos by the Lancashire Dynamo Company. By the time of its opening, the total length of mains cable, including feeders and distributors, but exclusive of street lighting and house service, was over nine miles, and the number of lamps ready for connection was 1,700.

Above: A milkman on his round at George Terrace on Stewart Avenue in the 1900s with, on the right, St Mary's Roman Catholic School on the corner into the Bog. Proposed in January 1902, the school opened on 1 September with a roll of 147 pupils under the care of three teachers, Miss Helen Donaghy, Miss Elizabeth Donaghy and Miss Sarah Donaghy, and closed in July 1954 when the headmaster, Mr Keith Fennie, transferred to St Anthony's School at Armadale and the pupils went to the new St Mary's Junior Secondary under Mr William Hall.

Left: A young girl making her way up the East Bog on a summer morning perhaps in the early 1950s. The Ordnance Survey map of 1856 shows it, and its parallel neighbour, as Eastern Bog and Western Bog, running on to South Street, and in his book *Borrowstouness and District*, Thomas J Salmon attributes the names to a spring water fed, swamp or marsh. Today their line is taken by Bomar Avenue.

Queen Ina, Grange School's first 'Queen', dressed for her coronation on. Friday, 14th July 1911 in Kinnigars Park. After her champion, Archie Buchanan, had thrown down his challenge – and none had accepted it – Ina was crowned by Lady Joan Verney, wife of Sir Harry Lloyd-Verney, then of Carriden. Born in April 1897, Thomasina Hamilton Ritchie was the daughter of Peter, a miner, and Margaret Ritchie of 18 Main Street (later moving to Mayfield Terrace). In December 1917 she married James Pegge Wilson, an electrician from Parkhead in Glasgow, then serving with the Gordon Highlanders.

George Learmonth, Champion to Queen Christina Blackwood (1903) of Borrowstoun School, on horseback in Stewart Avenue, beneath the partially completed town hall. He was the son of George G Learmonth of Northbank Farm, Carriden, whilst she lived at 83 Loudens Row with her mother, also Christina. The sword then carried by the Champion had been that of Admiral Sir James Hope (1808-1881), son of Admiral Sir George Hope-Vere and Lady Jemima Hope Johnstone.

The Bo'ness Co-operative Society's wagon, in their yard at Rattray Street, with Little Bo-Peep, re-united with at least two of her sheep, and ready to take part in a Fair Day Procession. The photograph is Edwardian and the man holding the horse is either John Johnston or William Neilson.

Another photograph from the 1900s, showing 'Hector the Horse' who took second place in the best dressed horse and cart section. As press reports name the entrant and not the horse it cannot be accurately dated

Left: Upper Forth Sailing Club members and their float, mounted on a model T Ford motor car, ready to join a children's fair parade in the 1920s. In February 1952 the Upper Forth Sailing Club joined with the Bridgeness Yacht Club and the Bo'ness Motor Cruising Club to form the Upper Forth Boat Club. An elegant silver cup presented to Bridgeness Yacht Club by J P Smith Esq. in 1907, and now on display in Kinneil Museum, is the earliest surviving club trophy. The oldest UFSC trophy is a cup presented by Thomas Blackadder Esq., its Vice Commodore, in 1925.

The Salvation Army Band leading part of the 1962 parade (Queen Elizabeth Murray) down Church Brae, followed by a Thomson & Balfour articulated lorry bearing the tableau 'Vienna Platz'. The front row of the band (left to right) is made up of Tom Stables, Trevor Martin, Alex Cook and Ian Angus, and in the second row are; Jim Robb, Robert Meldrum, Ernie Hodgson and John Spowart.

The coal merchant, John Henderson (on the right) with an employee and his lorry, on Grahamsdyke Road, decorated for the 1932 Fair Day (Queen Helen Burnett) – he won the best dressed light motor vehicle class. The cupolas and "St Paul's" would suggest the London cathedral but nothing suggests a Bo'ness connection. At the turn of the century Henderson lived in Hamilton Square with his parents, Robert (born Linlithgow) and Rachel (ms Gibb, born Bo'ness) who had married in 1868, and his siblings; William, a sawmill worker and Agnes, Margaret, Hugh and Rachel, all pottery workers. John never married, and was a coal miner until starting his own business as a coal merchant. He died at 64 Forthbank Square in October 1949, aged 78 years.

Born at Low Valleyfield, Fife in 1859, David Kennedy Harrower left the teaching profession at the early age of 16 years and came to Bo'ness seeking a commercial career. He joined the shipping agents Messrs John Denholm as a clerk and resigned, as a partner, in 1909 to found Messrs Harrower, Welsh & Co., pitwood importers and shipping agents at Kinneil Woodyard. With his experience at Denholm's, Harrower handled the pitwood side of the business, whilst Welsh, who died in 1911, handled the shipping. The firm grew and imported wood from not only the Baltic but from Spain and Newfoundland. In public life, Mr Harrower was vice-consul for the Netherlands, consular agent for Estonia and Belgium, a justice of the peace, chairman of West Lothian Unionist Association and chairman of the Bo'ness Gas Light Co. He died in March 1928.

Kinneil Miners' Welfare Institute at Castlehill shortly after its opening in November 1923. Designed by the Glasgow architects Thomson, Sandilands and McLeod, it consisted of a 400 seat hall / cinema, billiard room, recreation rooms and baths, with a caretaker's house, and provided miners with a means of social well-being and recreation. With 800 miners in the Kinneil district, this was the first of the larger type of miners' welfare institutes in Scotland, and cost £4,000 (including £3,000 from central funds). It would serve three generations of miners.

Kinneil Miners Welfare Institute, Bo' Ness

Christina Stanners, nee Cairns, with her daughters Mary and Agnes, possibly outside their home at Furnace Row. In December 1905, Christina, a 20 year old woodyard worker and 23 year old miner, William Martin Stanners were married at Carriden Manse by the Rev. William Dundas. Their first daughter, Mary was born at Miller Pit Cottages in June 1906, and in 1930 married John Hempseed Duff, a 26 year old railway guard. She died at Whitburn in 1979. Born in December 1908, whilst the family were at 10 Philpingstone Road, Agnes, like her mother and sister would work in one of the woodyards. In August 1930 she married Frederick Aitken Freer Quarrie, a 25 year old woodyard labourer, and died in 1998 aged 89 years.

Furnace Yard Pit and its bing. In 1845, the ironmaster John Wilson of Dundyvan, Lanarkshire, sank the Snab Pit – its 200 fathom (1200 feet) shaft being the costliest and deepest at that time – and in the early 1850s opened the Kinneil Ironworks, having discovered, accidentally, black band ironstone. The Kinneil Cannel and Coking Coal Co. sunk the new Furnace Yard Pit in 1892 that, in 1925, was taken over by the Lochgelly Iron and Coal Co. It went into liquidation in 1933 but Kinneil survived and worked on until Nationalisation in 1947.

A 1955 aerial view of Kinneil Colliery, with development work nearing completion. The bing was the product of its predecessors, the immediate being the Furnace Yard Pit (1020 feet), No. 2 Snab (1150 feet), No. 4 Snab (420 feet) and Lothians (642 feet). The new shafts would reach a depth of almost 3,000 feet.

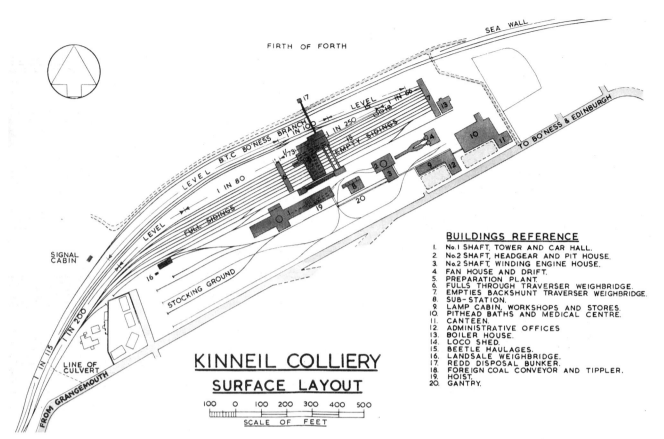

FIRTH OF FORTH

SEA WALL

KINNEIL COLLIERY

SURFACE LAYOUT

100 0 100 200 300 400 500
SCALE OF FEET

BUILDINGS REFERENCE

1. No.1 SHAFT, TOWER AND CAR HALL.
2. No.2 SHAFT, HEADGEAR AND PIT HOUSE.
3. No.2 SHAFT, WINDING ENGINE HOUSE.
4. FAN HOUSE AND DRIFT.
5. PREPARATION PLANT.
6. FULLS THROUGH TRAVERSER WEIGHBRIDGE.
7. EMPTIES BACKSHUNT TRAVERSER WEIGHBRIDGE.
8. SUB-STATION.
9. LAMP CABIN, WORKSHOPS AND STORES.
10. PITHEAD BATHS AND MEDICAL CENTRE.
11. CANTEEN.
12. ADMINISTRATIVE OFFICES
13. BOILER HOUSE.
14. LOCO SHED.
15. BEETLE HAULAGES.
16. LANDSALE WEIGHBRIDGE.
17. REDD DISPOSAL BUNKER.
18. FOREIGN COAL CONVEYOR AND TIPPLER.
19. HOIST.
20. GANTRY.

The surface layout of the new Kinneil Colliery. Designed by the National Coal Board's architect Egon Riss, Kinneil was one of their largest reconstructions, connecting, under the Forth, with Valleyfield Colliery in Fife in 1965.

The headgear of No. 2 shaft under construction. The first sod of the new colliery was turned by the Countess of Balfour, wife of Lord Balfour, chairman of the NCB (Scotland), on 25th June 1951. The Cementation Co. Ltd. then started the work of sinking the two 22 feet diameter concrete lined shafts, completing No. 1, at a depth of 2,877 feet on 8th March 1956, and No. 2 on 19th September to a depth of 2,886 feet, with insets at 1,269 feet, 1,824 feet and 2,274 feet. Pilot boreholes were always kept 30 feet ahead, but very little water was encountered as the work progressed through whinstone and volcanic ash.

An overview of the colliery from No. 1 Winding Tower in June 1957 with, on the right, the Grangemouth road leading into Bo'ness. Three years later it would reach its peak production level of 3,000 tons of coal per day with a workforce of 1,268. It closed on 14th December 1982 due to severe geological faults.

The Car Hall looking towards the shaft. Cars of coal, or stone, were directed to the appropriate tippler, and a weighing machine registered the output of coal.

The North British Railway C class locomotive 9675 (re-numbered 5244 by the LNER in 1946) with a goods wagon at Kinneil Engine Shed (64E), west of the Snab, in the late 1930s. The model was introduced in 1888, and this locomotive, built by Neilsons of Glasgow in 1891, worked until 1957. When Kinneil Shed closed in September 1952 the stock was transferred to Polmont from where it continued working the harbour and mines at Bo'ness and Kinneil.

Kinneil Signal Box, under the shadow of the bing to the right, in December 1955, was of typical North British Railway, red brick, construction (the other style being timber, such as the signal box at Birkhill). It was demolished and replaced in September 1961, by British Railways, but its successor lost its roof on the stormy night of 28th January 1968.

The North British Railway, Class C, locomotive, No. 9657, built at Cowlairs in 1891 (renumbered 5233 by the LNER in 1946), under the footbridge at Kinneil Signal Box, perhaps, in the late 1930s. With it are the driver J. Carson, the Fireman J. Martin, Guard P. Wales and Signalman R. Horn with the single line tablet over his shoulder. It was requisitioned for the period of the Great War and returned from France, bearing the name 'Plumer', in honour of Field Marshall Herbert Charles Onslow Plumer (1857-1932).

Signalman R Horn at Kinneil Signal Box in the 1930s.

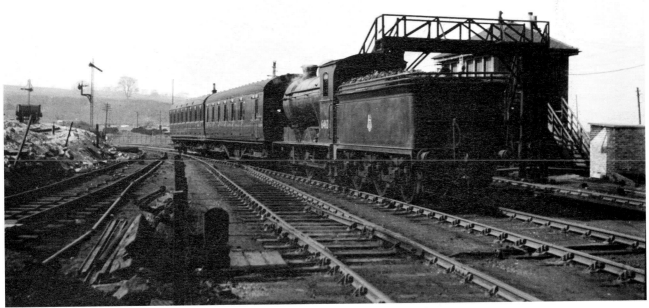

The 9.34am from Polmont to Bo'ness passing Kinneil signal box on 21st April 1956. With no turntable, the train was pushed this way and pulled on the return. The locomotive is a British Railways Class J37, No. 64636 based at St Margaret's Sheds, Edinburgh.

Built by Hawthorn Leslie of Newcastle upon Tyne in 1916 this Pug, or shunting locomotive, (works No. 3175) is thought to have started its working life with the ICI explosives plant at Billingham in County Durham and came to Kinneil in the early 1950s, for the opening of the new colliery. It was scrapped in 1962.

The Class J37 locomotive, No. 64636, hauling the 10.10am train out of Bo'ness for Polmont on 21st April 1956, and approaching Crawyett Bridge with Calder's yard on the left, and Kinneil Bing beyond. Calder processed and creosoted telegraph poles and railway sleepers.

Pug No. 41 (works No. 1107), photographed on 17th June 1968, was built at Andrew Barclay's Caledonia Works in Kilmarnock and dispatched, 10th June 1907, to the Lochgelly Iron & Coal Co. in Fife, where it remained until coming to Kinneil in 1967, from where it was scrapped in 1972. The driver is thought to be James Spiers.

Pug '41' with a train of empty wagons passing Kinneil bing.

A British Railways diesel electric locomotive (No. 20099) pulling out from the Preparation Plant at Kinneil.

In contrast to the brick built signal box at Kinneil, the one at Birkhill was of timber – with less weight there was less chance of subsidence. Opened on 13th August 1899, it survived until 23rd June 1957 and served not only as a passing loop but controlled access to the clay mine. To its right, under the paraffin lamp, is the platform for exchanging the single line token.

The Avenue, Kinneil Estate, photographed in 1925. Under powers granted by the Public Parks (Scotland) Act, 1875 – enabling local authorities in Scotland to acquire and lay out land for public parks and pleasure grounds in large overcrowded towns – the town council bid for Kinneil Estate in June 1922 and by the following August had a putting green on the front lawn.

Now a scheduled ancient monument, Kinneil House probably dates from the 1470s, when it was built by James, 1st Lord Hamilton – and partly blown up by the Earl of Morton a century later. When bought by Bo'ness Council – its lands to be a public park – they planned its demolition, but whilst the interior was being stripped, important early wall paintings were discovered, and it was restored. Between 1764 and 1794 it was the home of Dr John Roebuck, founder of the Carron Iron Works, and in the grounds is the ruin of the small house where James Watt worked on perfecting his steam engine in or around 1768.

Top: The view, east, along Grangepans, around 1910. The first opening on the left was unnamed, whilst second was Man of War Street (today's Man o' War Street), opposite the Crown Inn, with its flag pole. Depending on the exact date, the licensee was either John Jeffrey or Robert Masson. Today (2009) the inn is the only building to have survived the extensive programme of demolition and redevelopment. Grangepans was one of four villages in the eighteenth century parish of Carriden, the others being; Bridgeness, Benhardpans and Blackness, and was a busy port before losing out to Bo'ness. In the 'New' Statistical Account (1834-1845), written by the Rev David Fleming, we learn that in 1834 Grangepans had six working saltpans producing 23,000 bushels per annum. The Winchester bushel, a volume measure of 18 1/2 inches in diameter by 8 inches deep, contained 2,150.42 cubic inches.

Centre: Grangepans looking west, with the Danish Dairy Company's premises in Brechin's Buildings, on the corner of Hamilton Street, on the right.

Left: A 1915 newspaper advertisement for the Danish Dairy Company.

BRIDGENESS MINERS WELFARE SCHEME, BO'NESS.

Opposite: Bridgeness and Carriden Miners' Welfare Club on Harbour Road, soon after its opening on 31st May 1924. It differed from the 'Welfare' at Kinneil, opened the previous November, for here, with a bowling green, tennis court and putting green, the emphasis was on outdoor activities. The money, £2,600, came from the District Welfare Committee for Lanarkshire, formed under provisions in the Mining Industry Act, 1920, which had miner's welfare responsibility for the Scottish area. Their funding came from a levy of 1d. on every ton of coal raised. In his speech at the opening, Mr George Burr (1875-1929) manager of the Carriden Coal Company thanked: Mr Cadell who had gifted the site, Bo'ness Iron Co. for the ironwork for the outside seats and tables, Messrs Thomson & Balfour for the woodwork for the seats, Messrs P & W McLellan for the putting green clubhouse, and Vale of Grange Football Club for the flagpole.

Bridgeness Harbour photographed from Bridgeness Tower in the 1880s or 1890s. In more recent times, a little confusion has arisen as to what the photograph shows. In the foreground is Bridgeness Colliery's Pit No. 5 (the winding gear can just be seen through the smoke), and not the Victoria Sawmills, which is out of view to the right. On the shore line is Pit No. 6. The obvious export cargo for the ships was coal and salt, as they imported pit props.

Opposite: Bridgeness No. 1 Pit Rescue Brigade with their equipment, photographed in the early twentieth century. Little is known of them as individuals, but one surviving copy of the photograph names them as: front row (left to right); George Carr, James Pender (Captain), J Armstrong (manager), W Nesbit, W Gibson (Vice Captain):back row; Sgt McCormick (Instructor), W Stanners and W A Smith (Assistant). The five 'rescuers' are wearing 'Meco' – Modern Engineering Company – breathing apparatus which, with its full face mask, meant that they could expect to work in, or under, water. The two tanks held 300 litres of oxygen at 120 atmospheres and, delivered at 2.3 litres per minute, would last for 130 minutes. The exhaled breath was purified as it passed through a cylinder of caustic soda peas. The lamps they hold are carbide – burning acetylene, produced by the reaction of water on calcium carbide. James Pender (front, second left) is holding the Haldane Box, used (by aid of its occupant) for detecting firedamp, afterdamp and whitedamp, the carbon monoxide left after an explosion. Dr John Scott Haldane (1860-1936) devised the box following a mining disaster in the Rhondda Valley of Wales in 1896, reasoning, correctly, that a small creature – canaries were chosen as their bright colour could be seen in low light – would succumb to the gas at low concentrations and fall off their perch. There was a small cylinder of oxygen to revive them. In 1986 the birds were superseded by electronic detectors. In front of the sandbag weighted stretcher lie simple rescue tools – picks, shovels, a saw and a cantilever first aid box.

The "Bonnie Brook" group, with their nameplate.

Opposite: P & W McLellan's workers aboard the 3,000 ton *SS Bonnie Brook* on its arrival at the yard in April 1938. Built for the United States Maritime Commission at Harriman, Pennsylvania in 1920, she had been laid up for some time before delivering a load of scrap metal to Grangemouth and coming to McLellan's, as the seventh American cargo vessel to be broken up on the Forth that year. The men are not named but in the centre of the second row is Joseph McVeigh, their manager. The Forth Shipbreaking Company had been a fairly modest concern, employing some 30 or 40 men when, in May 1905, it took its first ship, *HMS Barracouta*, an obsolete man-o'-war, and remained small until the arrival of the surrendered German U-boats in 1919. In the following 30 years, under McVeigh, an Ulsterman who had trained with Harland and Wolff at Belfast, it was to break 135 vessels. In 1921 the company merged with P & W McLellan of Glasgow. McVeigh's eldest son Joseph, a shipping clerk, was a 21 year old 2nd Lieutenant with the Black Watch when he was killed on the Western Front on 28 March 1918, and buried at Arras.

Work progressing on the breaking of the six gun, twin screw, cruiser *HMS Barracouta*, the first ship to be broken up at Bridgeness, where she was beached in May 1905. Launched at the Royal Naval Dockyard, Pembroke in May 1889, she had a displacement of 1580 tons, a length of 233 feet, a beam of 35 feet and was armed with two, three gun turrets, and torpedoes. Also in her class were the *Barrosa*, the *Blanche* and the *Blonde* and although they were intended for the Far East service they spent their service life patrolling the Mediterranean.

Opposite: Of the 375 U-boats (Unterseeboot) built for the Kaiserliche Marine (German Imperial Navy) during World War One, 170 were surrendered to the Allies at the Armistice in November 1918, as prizes of war. The British Government sold their quota to breakers around the coast, and ten were purchased by the Forth Shipbuilding Company. These are the first six to arrive at Bridgeness, having been towed from Rosyth Dockyard, during the last weekend of March 1919, and the first work at the yard since August 1914. They consisted of the following;

U 62: Commissioned in December 1916, carried out nine patrols and sank 47 allied ships with a total tonnage of 123,294.
U 70: a type U66, (fourth from the left) commissioned in September 1915 from the Germaniawerft Shipyard at Kiel. It had a length of 228 feet, a beam of 21 feet, a submerged displacement of 933 tons, and was armed with twelve torpedoes (four tubes in the bow and one in the stern) and an 88mm gun. During its twelve patrols, it sank 53 allied ships with a total tonnage of 138,075. On 11th November 1918, with its crew of 35, it was surrendered by its commander, Kapitanleutnant Joachim Born.
U 94: Commissioned in March 1917, thirteen patrols, 20 ships sunk, tonnage 61,511.
UB 28: Commissioned in January 1916, no patrols.
UB 92: Commissioned in April 1918, two patrols, eight ships sunk, tonnage 18,628.
UC 59: Commissioned at the Kaiserliche Werft Shipyard at Danzig in May 1917, the UC 59 (second from the right, with the tarpaulin around the conning tower)) was a coastal minelayer, armed with only seven torpedoes, two tubes fore and one aft. She had two commanding officers; Herbert Lefholz (July to December 1917) and Oberleutnent Walter Strasser, who surrendered her. She had carried out nine patrols and sunk seven allied ships, with a total tonnage of 4,791. A further four U boats were later brought from Campbeltown in Argyllshire:
U 90: Commissioned in August 1917, seven patrols, 27 ships sunk with tonnage of 72,652.
UB 96: Commissioned in July 1918, one patrol, no successes.
U 96: Commissioned in April 1917, nine patrols, 31 ships sunk, tonnage 95,215.
UB 111: Commissioned in April 1918, three patrols, seven ships sunk, tonnage 694.

The 27,132 gross ton *SS Columbia* at McLellan's in 1936 with the 1903 built *SS Heracles* berthed in front of her. Launched from Harland & Woolf's yard at Belfast in 1914 she was laid up until 1917 when, aided by a government subsidy, she was fitted out and sold to the White Star Line of Liverpool as the *Belgic*. In 1918 she was refitted as a troop transport, again laid up, and refitted at Belfast, to appear as the *Belgenland* with the Red Star Line in 1923. Ten years later she was again laid up, for two years, before going to the Atlantic Transport Company of New York, who renamed her *Columbia*. The venture proved unprofitable and she was sold for scrap. A ship such as the *Columbia* was not just an iron hulk, she had been a luxury liner, and her fittings and contents held high value. The week before, P. & W. McLellan's head office at 129 Trongate, Glasgow, was advertising the nine day sale (commencing each day at 11.00am) of; The Most Important and Extensive Sale of the Luxurious and Costly Furnishings, Panelling and Equipment of the *TSS Columbia*, including electro-plated table appointments, and choice and costly furnishings from the dining-room, drawing room, lounges, smoking-rooms, cafes, cocktail bars and Japanese tea gardens.

Carriden House, set in 737 acres, including its three farms – Home, Stacks and Walton – was the parish's principal seat, dating from 1602 when it was built by Sir John Hamilton of Letterick. In 1814 it was bought by Admiral Sir George Johnstone Hope who was succeeded by his son Admiral Sir James Hope (1808-1881). His widow, Elizabeth Cotton (1842-1922), stayed on for a short time before re-marrying. She was followed by Sir James' sister, Helen Hope, and on her death in 1890, it passed to a nephew, Colonel George Lloyd Verney, the second son of Sir Harry Verney of Clayton, Buckinghamshire and to his eldest son James in 1909. In April 1915, when owned by a Mrs Constant of London, the house became a convalescent hospital for wounded soldiers – with eight beds in the drawing room and a further four in the dining room.

The gardener's house at Carriden in 1900, when occupied by 43 year old William Brand, from Dunbarney in Perthshire, and his Markinch born wife, Janet. They had not long moved here from Torphichen, bringing with them their children; Margaret (17), who was a kitchen maid in Carriden House, Charles (14), an apprentice plumber, eleven year old Jessie, nine year old Johann, and Catherine aged six.

Designed in the Norman style by the Glasgow architect Peter MacGregor Chalmers (1859-1922) and built of white Kinneil stone by local builders and quarrymasters, Peattie & Wilson, the foundation stone of Carriden Parish Church was laid by the Duke of Hamilton (Alfred Douglas, 13th Duke, 1862-1940) on Saturday 3rd October 1908 and opened the following September. The final cost of £6,100, including £600 for the 120 feet tower, would, using the retail price index, translate to £469,622 today (2009). From the old church was brought the bell dating from 1674 made by Pieter Oostens of Rotterdam and the Carriden Sea Box Society's model ship *Ranger*.

Carriden Colliery in the 1930s. The Carriden Coal Company began sinking the two 450 feet shafts in 1914 and the colliery remained in their hands until taken over by Bairds and Scottish Steels Ltd in May 1941. In its peak production year, 1948, its workforce of 316 produced 270 tons of coal per day (70,000 tons per year), but closure came in 1953 and it was abandoned in 1954. It is not known when these photographs were taken. Two hutches are on the ramp whilst a third is turning into the washer, where its contents would run on conveyors for pickers to removes stones. After washing it was dropped into the railway wagons on the track below.

Opposite upper: The pit head with its head frame and to the left the bottom of the ramp.

Opposite lower: Mr Christopher Jones, pit overseer, with some of his staff at Carriden Colliery in late 1940s.

Bo'ness scavengers (early refuse collectors), from left to right: Harry Smith, unknown, Willie Bracegirdle and Watty Turnbull aboard their truck on Castleloan Brae around 1926, heading for the tip. Behind them is the old Co-op building. The vehicle is an FWD model B truck, produced by the Four Wheel Drive Auto Co. at Clintonville, Wisconsin (where they still build fire engines) and used by the US Army as a general service truck. Between 1912 and the 1930s, 16,000 of them were built, the American Army bringing them to the war in Europe in 1917. After the war many were sold in Britain and adapted to various uses. They had a three speed gear box, solid rubber tyres on cast iron wheels, a 30 gallon capacity petrol tank and a top speed of fourteen mph. It was bought by the town council in 1920 as a successor to an electric wagon, found to be unsuitable for the town's hills. The men would have been paid between 46/- and 51/6d for their 48 hour week equivalent to about £300 to £350 in today's terms.

Opposite: A Leyland Tiger platform lorry at the coachbuilder John Stewart of Kirk Road, Wishaw in 1938, ready for delivery to William H Boyd of Corbiehall. But, all is not as it seems ... – the 'lorry' shown above, is now a bus. Boyd was a haulage contractor and bus operator and this adaptation, where the lorry platform was lifted off and the bus body hoisted on, although common during the Great War, was less popular by the late 1930s. What had delivered your bricks and mortar on Friday, could have taken you on a trip on the Saturday.

Founded in 1894 Bo'ness Pipe Band gave their first concert in the Volunteer Hall the following November. They opened the programme with a capital rendering of *Blue Bonnets*, and were followed by two soloists, a Miss Steel and Mr John Jeffrey who sang *Jessie's Dream* and *The Outlaw*. Bo'ness and Carriden Band made a contribution and Messrs Anderson and Campbell performed a number of step dances. And, Professor Wright, elocutionist, contributed a number of readings – an evening not have been missed. In 1919 the band members joined the Bo'ness Federation Pipe Band, with pipemajor Willie McComb in charge. This photograph is undated but the pipers in the back row are named as (left to right); Bruce Kidd, Charlie Stewart, Cherry Thomson, Dan McIntosh and John Smith, with John Stevenson on the bass drum.

Mary Hopkins Gilmour in highland dancing dress, at around eight years of age. Born in 1908 when her parents, John and Theresa (nee Devlin), lived in North Street, – her twin brothers James and John followed in June 1912, and they later moved to Marchlands Terrace. Her dancing brought her many successes and she was a talented musician, playing the piano, the guitar and the zither. She never married and retired, as a manageress, from the Hosiery Company around 1968 and passed away in 1978, aged 69 years.

The members of one or, perhaps, representatives of all three lodges of the Ancient Order of Free Gardeners in Bo'ness – Flowers of the Forest (No. 36), Rose of Grange (No. 30), and Pansy Blossom (No. 179) – around 1900. A nationwide organisation, akin to the Free Masons, the Gardeners was a friendly society, raising funds to support their members in times of sickness or disability and assisting with funeral expenses. Little is recorded of the Flowers of the Forest, whilst the Rose of Grange, founded in 1866, was dissolved in 1908. The Pansy Blossom, however, flourished and in May 1923 opened a first floor hall above the shops in Hope Street rounding into North Street.

Councillor Robert Ross at the time of his appointment as Provost of Bo'ness in May 1963. A foreman painter with West Lothian Council, he was elected to Bo'ness Town Council in 1952 (South Ward), and served as a councillor, junior baillie, honorary treasurer and provost. In 1964, following the reorganisation of the wards, due to the burgh extension, he contested the newly formed Graham Ward against three independent candidates, but was defeated. He also served on the board of Bo'ness Co-operative Society, was a founder member of the local branch of the British Legion, a stalwart member of Craigmailen Church and a keen Bo'ness United supporter. He was taken unwell at his home in Deanfield Crescent in December 1966 and died in Bangour Hospital.

Founded in 1911, due mainly to the drive of John Jeffrey, Bo'ness Amateur Operatic Society staged its first production, *HMS Pinafore*, in the spring of 1912, *The Pirates of Penzance* the following year and *The Mikado* in 1914. This was a time when many amateur companies were formed around the country to perform the works of Gilbert and Sullivan.

HIPPODROME, BO'NESS.

Sole Proprietor · · · · LOUIS D. DICKSON.

___

GIGANTIC SUCCESS.

LAST TWO NIGHTS

(FRIDAY AND SATURDAY)

of the Grand Production:

"MIKADO'

(By permission of Mr R. D'Oyly Carte)

BY THE

BO'NESS AMATEUR OPERATIC SOCIETY.

___

SIR ROBERT MURRAY,

Hon. President of the Society,

will preside on Saturday Evening.

___

TO-NIGHT at 8.   SATURDAY at 7-30.

ADMISSION—2/-, 1/6, 1/-, and 6d.

Full Particulars—See Bills.

J. C., Secy.

Mr JOHN JEFFREY as "Pooh-Bah."

Sketched in Hippodrome.

A prominent Character in the "Mikado" production last week

A pen and ink sketch of Mr John Jeffrey as Pooh-Bah, the pompous and ostentatious, 'Lord High Everything Else' - holding many offices and fulfilling none of them - in the 1914 production of *The Mikado*. Mr Jeffrey, the *Bo'ness Journal* reported, somewhat unkindly, *had a part that suited him.*

The principal players in the 1914 Bo'ness Amateur Operatic Society production, *The Mikado*, staged in the Hippodrome in the last week of March. Only Mr John Morrison, as the Mikado (centre front) has been positively identified. Amongst those with him are; Nanki-Poo (Mr E Russell McMillan), Lord High Executioner Ko-Ko (Mr R G Sheehan), Lord High Everything Else, Pooh-Bah (Mr John Jeffrey) and the Noble Lord Pish-Tush (Mr Thomas Dawson). The Bo'ness Journal's report of the first night's production is cool – *The first performance was given on Wednesday evening to an audience, which left something to be desired* – although the report praises the players individually.

The society assembled on the Town Hall stage during their production of *The Yeoman of the Guard*, between 7th and 10th March 1923. Members also performed choral work, at least once winning the Maconochie Cup at the West Lothian Choral Festival, at Linlithgow, in May 1930.

The principal players in *The Yeoman of the Guard* with (from left to right) Mr William Chalmers, *Colonel Fairfax*; Mr John Jeffrey, *Wilfred Shadbolt*; Mrs P M Monteith, *Phoebe Meryll* and Mr George Vallance as *Jack Point*.

A newspaper advertisement for *The Yeoman of the Guard* production in March 1923.

BO'NESS AMATEUR OPERATIC SOCIETY.

GRAND PRODUCTION
of Gilbert & Sullivan's Celebrated Comic Opera:

"THE YEOMEN OF THE GUARD"
(By permission of R. D'Oyly Carte, Esq.)

TOWN HALL, BO'NESS,
(For FOUR NIGHTS)

Wednesday, Thursday, Friday, Saturday,
7th, 8th, 9th and 10th MARCH.

FULL BAND and CHORUS of 90 PERFORMERS.
LIVELY HUMOUR!   SPARKLING MUSIC!   HAUNTING CHORUSES!
Accompaniments by BO'NESS AMATEUR ORCHESTRAL SOCIETY.

Doors Open at 7.30 ;   Early Doors for Ticket-Holders at 7.15.
Curtain each evening at 8 o'clock prompt.
TICKETS (inclusive of Tax)   ...   ...   3/- (Reserved), 2/- and 1/-
Booking Plan with Mr ALEX. FRASER, Chemist, Hope Street, Bo'ness.

There are many surviving copies of this photograph, purporting to show the Old Raw (Row) (Tree) Blues as winners of the King Cup (presented by Leith sports shop proprietor Percival King) in 1884, including the one from which this image was taken. The board on which this copy is mounted names the team as:

Front row: Auld and W Campbell.

Middle row: unknown (the bottom left corner broken off), M McQueen, B Sneddon, W Bow (possibly William Bow, (32), coal miner, 19 Linlithgow Row), P Mair and C Grant.

Back row: T Grieve (possibly Thomas Grieve, (21), grocer, Roseneath Cottage), D Grant, D Burden (possibly David Burden, (24), ironworks labourer, 37 Furnace Row) and A Neil.

It is also inscribed 'Old Row Tree Blues Bo'ness'. There are, however, difficulties with the veracity of the inscription – it is not known when the names, or the information, was added. What is more likely, is that it shows Bo'ness (founded 1881) in their blue shirts and white shorts, after beating Broxburn Shamrock 4 – 0 to win the Edinburgh Football Association Consolation Cup on Saturday, 24 May 1884.

Opposite upper: A studio photograph of Bo'ness Wednesday Football Club, in their green and white, in the 1890s. Throughout the country there were many 'Wednesday' clubs, composed of shopkeepers and their assistants who worked Saturdays – locally, there was Queensferry, Armadale, Bathgate and Broxburn. Bo'ness may have played at Calder Park.

Opposite lower: Bo'ness Football Club's team in the season 1924-25 when they won the Linlithgowshire FA Cup. They are named as:

Front row: H Goodwin, Charlie Martin, Johnny Rayne, Tommy Cottingham and C Kelly;

Middle row: T Anderson, M McDonald, S Milligan, H Girvan, Billy Moffat and C Cook;

Back row: W Stewart, P Brown, P Graham, J Miller (committee members).

On the left is manager A Wyllie and on the right, trainer D Cunningham.

An early photograph of Bo'ness Bowling Club members assembled in front of the original clubhouse. The founding members, wholly composed of leading citizens and business men in the burgh, numbered 110 who, on the club being made a limited company (with capital of £500), became shareholders, with John Marshall, solicitor, of Craigderroch and South Street, as president. The ground on Grange Terrace was bought, and the bowling green contractor, Daniel Leslie of Brownswood, Bishopbriggs, near Glasgow, engaged to lay the green. The balance sheet at the end of the first year showed a modest £28.9.7 on the right side, with an overdraft of £100.9.1. due to their less than modest clubhouse, costing £128.11.2. It opened on Saturday, 14th June 1902, when Mrs John Marshall threw the first jack.

Wednesday 30th April 1930 and Mr John Sneddon stands by as Mrs R Taylor throws a long jack to open Bo'ness Bowling Club's new season. She was presented with a silver jack on an ebony stand. Thanking the club on her behalf, Mr Taylor said that as wives tended to think their husbands spent too much time on the bowling green, he could now reply that he was endeavouring to bring success to what she had started. The roller on the left of the photograph is still in service.

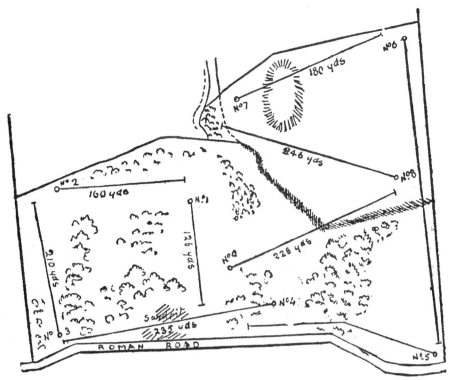

The layout plan of West Lothian Golf Club's course, published for its opening on Christmas Day 1892. With a year of work behind them, and a membership of 80, Sheriff George Fisher Melville of Linlithgow played the first ball. The nine hole course had been laid out by Willie Park (1864-1925) of Musselburgh, winner of the Open Championship (1887 and 1889) – as had his father, Willie Park Snr and his uncle, Mungo Park – who thought of the course that, what is wanted in extent is eminently made up for by the sporting qualities of the ground. His expertise was responsible for the design of over 170 courses in Europe, America and Canada including the famous Sunningdale Course in Berkshire. The Sheriff's first shot brought applause and a cheer before play, in pairs, started. One little problem was the keenness of the frost, and the difficulties experienced by those playing white balls as opposed to those playing red ones.

Members of West Lothian Golf Club (founded 1892) assembled and photographed by Mr D Stewart of Bo'ness, to celebrate the opening of their new clubhouse by Mr H M Cadell, on Saturday, 2nd July 1898. Seated, in the centre, will be Mr Cadell with Mr J C Liddle, solicitor, the Club Secretary and Mr William Russell, solicitor, the Club Captain. The clubhouse building was supplied and built by R R Speirs & Co of Glasgow, specialists in prefabricated timber framed buildings.

The Co-operative Society's annual social evening and dance in the town hall on Tuesday, 22nd February 1938. After tea, and a speech by the chairman Mr James Black, the company of 300 were entertained by Mr William Waddell of Falkirk's concert party and danced to the music of Tom Stewart's band. Between times they found time for a whist drive.

The Pageants, a Bo'ness charity group that raised funds for Edinburgh Royal Infirmary, through parades and events. They have been named as:
Front row: (left to right); Meikle(?), Sinclair, William Greenhorn, unknown and Mulholland.
Centre row: McAlpine, Joe Murray (Derry Close, Grangepans), Findlay, Sinclair and unknown.
Back row: Meikle, unknown, unknown. Some of the moustaches are false, owing their appearance to soot.

The cast of the 1950 or 1951 Public School Pantomime, an annual production at the town hall, produced by Josephine Turnbull.

Early twentieth century employees of the shipbrokers and timber merchants, John Denholm & Co. of Custom House Buildings, named on the original photograph as; A Baird, J Docherty, S Docherty, Terry, Gourlay, Muir and Calderwood.

A group of workers, thought to be at Ballantyne's Foundry, in the late 1930s who are named as:
Front row: unknown, unknown, unknown and Pinny Docherty.
Back row: Joseph Docherty, George Docherty, James Lowrie and Johnny Docherty.